Savoury Sp[...] from **Alsace**

...vours of yesterday and today

by

Didier ROECKEL
and his team

photos by

Frédérique CLEMENT

I. D. L'Édition

Contents

APERITIF

Bretzel   4

Savoury Kougelhof   6

SOUPS

Onion soup   8

Split pea soup   8

Asparagus cream   10

STARTERS AND LIGHT DISHES

Terrine   12

Pot au feu salad   14

Onion tart   16

Alsatian-style snails   18

Potato pancakes   20

Presskopf   22

Black pudding in puff pastry   24

Duck foie gras   26

Strasbourg salad   28

MAIN COURSES

Baeckeoffe   30

Savoury vol-au-vents   32

Fleischnaka   34

Lamb fries in Riesling   36

Braised salted pork riblets with turnips   38

Surlawerlas   40

Jugged venison   42

Pheasant with sauerkraut 44

Stuffed pig's stomach 46

Sauerkraut (Choucroute) 48

Tarte flambée 50

Kassler 52

Munster casserole 54

Crispy pig's trotter 56

Knuckle of ham with Munster 58

Calf's head 60

Young cockerels in Riesling 62

Braised pork cheeks 64

Roosbif 66

Sauerkraut pie 68

Pot au feu 70

Liver dumplings 72

FISH

Fried carp 74

Fish stew 76

Zander in Riesling 78

Sauerkraut with fish 80

Zander cordon bleu 82

SIDE DISHES

Spaetzle 84

Fromage blanc dumplings 84

Damfnudel 86

Potato salad 86

Bretzel

Preparation: 15 min
Proving time: 2 hours
Cooking: 15 min

For 6 bretzels

- 500 g flour
- 20 g fresh yeast
- 15 g salt
- 30 cl milk
- 30 g butter
- 2 egg yolks

For the soaking:

- 1.5 l water
- 40 g bicarbonate of soda

Make a well in the flour, add the salt, the crumbled yeast, the milk and the softened butter in small pieces. Knead together until you have a smooth dough. Shape into a ball and cover the dish with a cloth.

Leave to rest until the dough has doubled in volume.

Divide the dough into 6 equal parts and roll them into sausage shapes 50 cm long and 1 centimetre in diameter.

Shape them into bretzels.

Bring 1.5 litres of water to the boil with the bicarbonate of soda.

Drop the bretzels into the boiling water and take them out again straight away.

Put them on greaseproof paper on an oven tray.

Brush with egg yolk and sprinkle with coarse salt and bake at 260°C, thermostat 9, for 15 minutes.

Kougelhof salé
Savoury Kougelhof

Preparation: 1 hour
Cooking: 40 min

Serves 6

- *500 g flour*
- *2 eggs*
- *20 g yeast*
- *20 cl milk*
- *100 g softened butter*
- *10 g salt*
- *150 g bacon*
- *1 onion*
- *110 g walnuts*

Roughly chop 30 g of walnuts.

Finely slice the bacon into lardons and the onion and then panfry them with no additional fat until the bacon is opaque. Set to one side.

Put the flour in a salad bowl and make a well in it. Add the beaten eggs, the crumbled yeast and the salt and gradually add the milk. Knead, then add the softened butter and knead again.

Add the bacon and the chopped walnuts and knead until you obtain a smooth dough.

Cover the salad bowl and put in a warm place until the dough doubles in volume.

Knead the dough again.

Butter and flour a kougelhof mould.

Arrange the rest of the walnuts in the bottom of the mould and add the dough.

Leave to rise in a warm place until the dough reaches the top of the mould.

Bake for an hour and 10 minutes at 170°C, thermostat 6.

Definition:

Softened butter: *Butter at room temperature.*

Serving suggestion: *Dry white wine.*

Soupe à l'oignon   Onion soup

Preparation: 30 min
Cooking: 30 min

Serves 6

- 1 kg onions
- 3 l beef stock
- 10 cl oil
- 18 slices of French baguette
- 150 g grated Gruyere

Heat the oil in a large saucepan.

Brown the onions.

Add the stock and cook over a low heat for 30 minutes.

While this is happening, dry the slices of bread in the oven at 180°C, thermostat 6, for around 5 to 6 minutes.

To serve the onion soup, arrange the slices of dried bread on top and sprinkle with grated Gruyere.

Soupe de pois cassés   Split pea soup

Preparation: 30 min
Cooking: 1 hour

Serves 6

- 600 g split peas
- 300 g smoked bacon
- 3 slices of bread
- 100 g carrots
- 100 g leeks
- 100 g onions
- 1 clove of garlic
- 100 g butter
- Salt, pepper

Peel and chop all the vegetables.

Heat the butter in a large saucepan and sweat the vegetables and the split peas.

Add 3 litres of water and cook for 1 hour over a low heat. Blend and season.

In a frying pan, brown the lardons and the croutons.

Sprinkle the lardons and the croutons over the soup.

Crème d'asperges
Asparagus cream

Preparation: 20 min
Cooking: 20 min

Serves 6

- *1 kg white asparagus*
- *50 g butter*
- *30 cl liquid cream*
- *Salt, pepper*
- *Chervil*

Peel the asparagus and cut them into 3-cm pieces.

Cook the asparagus for 10 minutes in 2 litres of boiling salted water.

Put the tips and the cooking water to one side.

Cut the rest of the asparagus into small pieces and sweat them in the butter.

Moisten with 1.5 litres of water and add the cream.

Season and blend.

Leave to cook for 10 minutes over a low heat.

Put the asparagus tips into the bottom of a soup tureen and pour over the velouté.

Terrine

Preparation: 45 min
Marinade: 24 hours
Cooking: 1½ hours

Für 1 Terrine

- *300 g sausage meat*
- *300 g pork fillet, chopped*
- *150 g pork fillet*
- *150 g turkey escalope*
- *150 g carrots*
- *50 g celeriac*
- *2 eggs*
- *10 cl red wine*
- *10 cl white wine*
- *15 g nitrite pickling salt*
- *2 bacon bards*
- *100 g duck mousse*

The day before

Cut the 150 g of pork fillet and the turkey escalope into strips.

Peel the carrots and the celeriac and cut them into julienne strips.

Mix all the ingredients except the bacon bards and the duck mousse.

Leave to marinate for 24 hours.

On the day

Make a cylinder the same length as the terrine dish with the duck mousse and wrap it with the bard.

Line a terrine dish with the bacon bards, allowing them to overlap over the edges of the terrine dish in order to cover the filling later.

Spread a third of the filling in the bottom of the terrine dish, tamp down and add the cylinder of duck mousse.

Cover with the rest of the filling and tamp down again.

Cover with the bacon bard. Cover with a sheet of aluminium foil and put the lid on the terrine dish.

Preheat the oven to 180°C, thermostat 6.

Cook in a bain marie for 1½ hours.

Serving suggestion: Green salad and crudités.

Definition:

Julienne: Cut the vegetables into strips around 3 mm thick and 4 or 5 long.

Line: Cover the sides of a mould.

Salade de pot au feu

Pot au feu salad

Preparation: 20 min

Serves 6

- 600 g cooked
  pot au feu meat
- 100 g cooked
  pot au feu vegetables
- 50 g onions
- 5-6 gherkins
- 50 g parsley
- 100 g sweet corn

For the vinaigrette

- 10 cl oil
- 5 cl vinegar
- 2 cl water
- 1 egg yolk
- 1 tbsp mustard condiment
- 1 tbsp horseradish
- Salt, pepper

Cut the meat and the vegetables into small dice.

Chop the gherkins and the parsley. Slice the onion.

Put all the ingredients in a salad bowl. Add the sweet corn.

Mix all the ingredients for the vinaigrette and pour into the salad bowl.

Mix and serve.

Tip: Use the leftovers from pot au feu.

Tarte à l'oignon
Onion tart

Preparation: 40 min
Cooking: 30 min
Resting time: 1 hour

Serves 6

For the pastry
- 250 g flour
- 125 g softened butter
- 1 pinch of salt
- 1 egg
- 2 tbsp water

For the filling
- 1 kg onions
- 100 g butter
- 100 g lardons
- 1 egg
- 60 g flour
- 3 dl milk
- Salt, pepper
- Nutmeg

Sift the flour and make a well in it. Add the beaten egg, the salt and the water and work together with some of the flour.

Add the diced butter and knead.

Roll it into a ball and leave to rest for one hour.

Peel and finely slice the onions.

Put them in a saucepan with the butter, cover and cook over a low heat for 10 minutes.

Sprinkle with flour, mix well and then add the milk. Season and add a pinch of nutmeg.

Cook for 5 minutes over a low heat.

Butter the tart tin.

Roll out the pastry, use it to line the tart tin and pour in the onion preparation.

Bake for 30 minutes at 220°C, thermostat 7.

Serving suggestion: green salad.

Definition:

Softened butter: *butter at room temperature.*

Roll out: *roll out the pastry.*

Line: *Cover the base of the tart tin with the pastry.*

Escargots à l'alsacienne

Alsatian-style snails

Preparation: 15 min
Cooking: 10 min

Serves 6

- *6x12 snails*
- *300 g butter*
- *12 g salt*
- *6 g pepper*
- *50 g parsley*
- *20 g garlic*
- *30 g shallots*
- *2 cl Ricard*
- *2 cl Worcester sauce*

Allow the butter to come to room temperature in order to soften it.

Finely chop the garlic, the shallots and the parsley.

Work all the ingredients into the butter to mix evenly.

Put the snails in a snail dish or in their shells and cover with butter.

Bake at 250°C for 10 minutes.

Serve as soon as the butter starts to bubble and foam.

Galettes de pommes de terre
Potato pancakes

Preparation: 20 min
Cooking: 15 min

Serves 6

- 1 kg potatoes
- 2 shallots
- 2 eggs
- 1 bunch of parsley
- 1 clove of garlic
- Salt, pepper

Peel and grate the potatoes.

Drain them in a sieve and press them to extract their liquid.

Finely chop the parsley and slice the shallots. Crush the garlic.

Beat the eggs with a whisk.

Season the potatoes and mix all the ingredients.

Heat a little oil in a frying pan.

Put small mounds of potato in the frying pan and flatten them with a spatula.

Cook until golden, around 7 minutes on each side.

Serve hot.

Serving suggestion: with a green salad.

Presskopf

Preparation: 45 min
Cooking: 3½ hours
Resting time before eating:
2 days

For 1 terrine

- *1 boned pig's head*
- *1 pig's tongue*
- *50 g carrots*
- *50 g celery*
- *50 g leeks*
- *50 g white cabbage*
- *50 g butter*
- *100 g chives*
- *1 l white wine*

Put the pig's head, the tongue and the white wine in a large saucepan and cover with water. Cook for 2½ hours.

Drain the meat and decant the cooking liquor. Strain it.

Peel the tongue and cut the meat into small pieces.

Peel the vegetables and cut them into small pieces.

Brown them in the butter. Add the pieces of meat and moisten with the cooking liquor.

Leave to cook for 20 minutes.

Chop the chives and add them at the end of cooking time.

Arrange the meat and the vegetables in a terrine dish and add enough cooking liquor to just cover the meat.

Put in the fridge and leave to rest for 2 days before eating.

Serving suggestion: Crudités, vinaigrette and onion rings.

Feuilleté de boudin

Black pudding in puff pastry

Preparation: 30 min
Cooking: 25 min

Serves 6

• 4 pieces of puff pastry
6 black puddings
3 Golden Delicious apples
1 pinch of cinnamon
1 teaspoon of sugar
2 egg yolks

Peel the apples and cut them into small pieces.

Add the cinnamon and the sugar to the apples. Mix.

Cut out 12 circles of puff pastry 12 cm in diameter.

Peel the black puddings.

Spread half of the apples on 6 circles of pastry, add a black pudding and cover with the rest of the apples.

Top with the remaining 6 circles of pastry and seal the edges of the pastry with the egg yolk.

Brush the pastry with egg yolk.

Arrange the individual pastries on an oven tray and bake for 25 minutes at 180°C, thermostat 6.

Check that the pastries are nicely browned before serving.

Serving suggestion: green salad.

Foie gras de canard
Duck foie gras

Preparation: 1 hour
Cooking: 45 min
Resting time: 12 hours
Resting time before eating:
2-3 days

Serves 6

- 1 raw foie gras weighing 600 g
- 4 g foie gras spice mixture
- 8 g salt
- 1 cl Port
- 1 cl Cognac
- 1 cl Ricard

For the onion jam
- 400 g onions
- 300 g sugar
- 50 cl red wine
- 1 teaspoon 4-spice mix

Leave the foie gras at room temperature for 1 hour so that it becomes pliable.

Spread open the lobes of the foie gras and remove any sinews by pulling gently on the veins.

Spread the salt, the spices and the alcohols over the foie gras.

Close up the foie gras and put it in a terrine into which it fits snugly.

Press lightly.

Put a sheet of aluminium foil over the surface of the foie gras before closing the terrine.

Leave to rest in the fridge for 12 hours.

Preheat the oven to 60°C, thermostat 2.

Put the terrine into a deep oven dish containing boiling water and put in the oven for 45 minutes.

Leave to cool and rest in the fridge for 2 to 3 days before eating.

For the onion jam

Peel and finely slice the onions.

Put all the ingredients for the onion jam in a saucepan and reduce over a low heat until the onions form a jam. Around 1½ hours.

Salade strasbourgeoise
Strasbourg salad

Preparation: 15 min

Serves 4

- 600 g Gruyere
- 4 saveloys
- 1 onion
- ½ bunch of parsley
- A few mesclun leaves

For the vinaigrette
- 4 tbsp oil
- 2 tbsp vinegar
- 1 egg yolk
- Salt, pepper

Finely chop the parsley. Peel the onion and slice it into fine rings on a mandolin.

Slice the Gruyere into fine strips on a mandolin. Cut the strips into tagliatelle lengthways.

Peel the saveloys, cut them in half lengthways and score widthways.

Mix all the ingredients for the vinaigrette.

Dress the salad, the Gruyere and the saveloys and sprinkle with parsley and onion rings.

Definition:

Mandolin: kitchen utensil used to slice vegetables in various thicknesses.

Mesclun: mixture of several varieties of salad.

Baeckeoffe

Preparation: 1 hour
Cooking: 3½ hours

Serves 6

- 1 kg pork loin
- 1 pig's trotter cut into rounds
- 500 g boned shoulder of mutton
- 500 g beef silverside
- 1.5 kg potatoes
- 300 g carrots
- 1 leek
- 200 g onions
- 1 l white wine
- Salt, pepper

Cut the meat into medium sized pieces, 5 to 6 cm.

Wash, peel and chop the potatoes, the leek and the carrots into rounds.

Slice the onions.

Butter the bottom of a terrine.

Cover the bottom with the onions and add one layer with half of the potatoes and one layer with half of the carrots. Season.

Arrange the meat and the rounds of pig's trotter on top. Season.

Cover with the rounds of leek, the rest of the carrots and the potatoes.

Pour in the wine until it comes half way up the side of the terrine. Cover and bake at 220°C, thermostat 7, for 3½ hours.

Bouchées à la reine
Savoury vol-au-vents

Preparation: 35 min
Cooking: 1 ½ hours

Serves 6

For the meat
- *1 chicken*
- *500 g veal chuck steak*
- *1 onion*
- *1 clove*
- *1 stick of celery*
- *1 carrot*
- *1 leek*
- *1 bouquet garni*

For the mushrooms
- *200 g mushrooms*
- *40 g butter*

For the sauce
- *1.5 l chicken stock*
- *20 cl cream*
- *1 egg*
- *90 g butter*
- *90 g flour*
- *Salt, pepper*

Bring 3 to 4 litres of water to boil in a large saucepan.

Peel the onion and stick the clove into it. Peel the carrot, clean the celery and the leek. Add all the ingredients for the meat to the stock.

Add the chicken and the chuck steak. Skim regularly. Simmer for 1 ¼ hours.

Remove the meat and allow to cool.

Debone the meat and cut into small pieces.

Wash and slice the mushrooms.

Melt the butter in a frying pan. Add the mushrooms and fry them for 5 minutes. Season. Put to one side.

Make a roux. To do this, melt the butter in a saucepan, add the flour and mix until it starts to colour. Add the stock gradually and reduce for 10 minutes.

Add the meat and the mushrooms. Reduce the heat so that it is no longer at the boil.

Beat the egg yolk with the cream and pour into the sauce to thicken it.

Pour into the sauce and mix.

Preheat the oven to 180°C, thermostat 6. Heat the vol-au-vents for 5 minutes.

Pour the mixture into the vol-au-vents and serve.

Serving suggestion: with rice, spaetzle.

Fleischnaka

Preparation: 1½ hours
Cooking: 20 min

Serves 6

- *600 g cooked pot au feu meat*
- *200 g cooked pot au feu vegetables*
- *2 eggs*
- *200 g parsley*
- *2 tbsp oil*
- *50 cl chicken stock*
- *10 cl white wine*
- *1 bay leaf*

For the pastry
- *500 g flour*
- *5 eggs*
- *1 tbsp vinegar*
- *Salt*

Put the sifted flour in a round-bottomed mixing bowl. Make a well in it and add the beaten eggs. Add the vinegar and a pinch of salt. Knead together until you obtain a thoroughly mixed, smooth, firm pastry. Leave to rest for 20 minutes.

Chop the meat, the vegetables and the parsley.

Mix together, adding 2 eggs. Correct the seasoning if necessary.

Roll out a rectangle of pastry 2 mm thick.

Spread the filling over the pastry, leaving one centimetre clear of filling to seal the pastry.

Roll up the pastry tightly and seal the centimetre of pastry to the roll with a little water.

Cut into 2-cm slices.

Heat the oil in a cast iron casserole dish and brown the portions on each side.

Add the stock, the wine and the bay leaf and cook for 10 minutes.

Serving suggestion: Marrowbone dumplings.

Tip: Use the leftovers from pot au feu.

Definition:

Roll out: roll out the pastry.

Rognons blancs au Riesling
Lamb fries in Riesling

Preparation: 20 min
Cooking: 30 min
Soaking: 24 hours

Serves 6

• *3 pairs of lamb fries*

• *1 L Milk*

• *200 g mushrooms*

• *15 g shallots*

• *15 g garlic*

• *30 cl crème fraîche*

• *20 cl Riesling*

• *30 cl veal stock*

• *Salt, pepper*

Cut the lamb fries lengthways, wash them in cold water and soak them in milk for 24 hours.

The next day, cut the lamb fries into 1-cm slices.

Slice the shallots and mushrooms.

Panfry the lamb fries in a knob of butter over a high heat for 3 minutes. Reduce the heat and add the shallots, the crushed garlic and the mushrooms. Soften for around 8 minutes until the cooking juices have reduced.

Deglaze with Riesling, reduce and add the crème fraîche and the veal stock.

Cook for 10 minutes over a low heat.

Definition:

Deglaze: dissolve the juices caramelised during cooking with a liquid.

Serving suggestion: accompany with rice or pasta.

Wine: Riesling.

Cotis salés, navets confits
Braised salted pork riblets with turnips

**Preparation: 20 min
Cooking: 1 hour 40 minutes**

Serves 6

- 1.5 kg salted turnips
- 2 kg salted pork riblets
- 700 g potatoes
- 100 g onions
- 50 cl white wine
- 5 cloves of garlic
- 2 bay leaves
- 3 cloves
- 1 tbsp oil or lard

Cook the salted riblets in water for 1 hour.

Put the cooking liquor to one side.

Leave to cool and cut into identical portions.

Slice the onions and brown them in the oil.

Add half of the turnips, the cloves, the bay leaf and the crushed cloves of garlic and cover with the remaining turnips.

Cover the turnips with the liquor in which the riblets were cooked and cook covered for 30 minutes.

Surlawerlas
Surlawerla (saure Schweineleber)

Preparation: 20 min
Cooking: 25 min

Serves 6

- 650 g pig's liver
- 100 g lardons
- 2 onions
- 25 cl white wine
- 80 g butter
- 10 cl vinegar
- 10 cl veal stock
- 10 g flour
- 1 bouquet garni
- Salt, pepper

Cut the liver into evenly sized pieces.

Chop the onions and brown them.

Add the pieces of liver and the lardons and brown.

Sprinkle with flour and leave to brown.

Moisten with the veal stock and the white wine.

Add the bouquet garni. Season.

Leave to simmer for 25 minutes over a low heat.

Add the vinegar, mix, check that it is cooked and correct the seasoning if necessary.

Serving suggestion: Green salad, spaetzle

Civet de cerf
Jugged venison

Marinade: 24 hours
Preparation: 20 min
Cooking: 1 ½ hours

Serves 6

• 1.5 kg shoulder of venison

For the marinade
• 1 l red wine
• 3 tbsp oil
• 1 onion
• 3 shallots
• 2 carrots
• 6 juniper berries
• 12 coriander seeds
• 10 peppercorns
• 1 bouquet garni
• 1 tbsp coarsely ground white peppercorns

For the cooking
• 50 g butter
• 1 tbsp oil
• 1 onion
• 1 bay leaf
• 50 g flour
• Salt, pepper

The day before

Cut the meat into 4-centimetre cubes.

Peel the onion, the shallots and carrots and roughly chop.

Mix the meat and the vegetables with the remaining ingredients for the marinade.

Marinate in the fridge for 24 hours.

The next day

Drain the meat.

Strain the marinade and keep 50 cl of the liquor.

Slice the onion.

Heat the oil and the butter and brown the meat.

Add the onion and sprinkle with flour.

Moisten with the liquor and add 25 cl of water.

Season.

Cover and cook over a low heat for 1 hour.

Serving suggestion: Spaetzle.

Faisan à la choucroute
Pheasant with sauerkraut

Preparation: 20 min
Cooking: 1 ½ hours

Serves 6

* 1 kg sauerkraut
* 1 onion
* 400 g smoked bacon
* 25 cl white wine
* 10 cl water
* 15 cl Cognac
* 2 bay leaves
* 2 cloves
* 5 juniper berries
* 50 g butter
* 12 breasts of pheasant
* Salt, pepper

Rinse the sauerkraut in cold water and then in warm water. Drain.

Slice the onion.

Cut the bacon in to large lardons.

Colour the onion and the lardons in a casserole dish.

Once coloured, cover with sauerkraut, add the spices and then the wine, the water and the Cognac.

Cook for one hour over a low heat.

Heat the butter and a teaspoon of oil in a frying pan and panfry the breasts for 3 minutes on each side.

Slice the breasts before serving.

Estomac de porc farci
Stuffed pig's stomach

Preparation: 1¼ hours
Cooking: 1½ hours

Serves 6

- 1 pig's stomach
- 400 g sausage meat
- 100 g turkey escalope
- 100 g veal escalope
- 150 g ice cubes
- 100 g carrots
- 100 g celery
- 100 g turnips
- 100 g leeks
- 200 g potatoes
- 1 l veal stock
- 30 cl water
- 30 cl white wine
- Salt, pepper

Peel and wash the vegetables and cut them into 1-centimetre dice.

Blanch them in a large quantity of boiling water for 5 minutes.

Wash the pig's stomach and rub the inside with coarse salt. Dry it.

Chop the pork, turkey and veal meat with the ice cubes.

Mix the chopped meat and the vegetables. Season.

Stuff the stomach and sew up the opening.

Poach the stomach in a large quantity of boiling water for 1 hour.

Once the stomach is poached, put it in a high-sided dish. Pour over the veal stock, the water and the wine and bake for 30 minutes at 180°C. The cooking liquor should come up to the mid point of the stuffed stomach.

Arrange it in a dish and pour over the sauce.

Serving suggestion: Green salad.

Choucroute
Sauerkraut

Preparation: 25 min
Cooking: 1 ½ hours

Serves 6

- *2 kg sauerkraut*
- *1 onion*
- *100 g lard*
- *1 bay leaf*
- *50 cl Riesling*
- *1 clove of garlic*
- *10 juniper berries*
- *4 coriander seeds*
- *Salt, pepper*

- *1 Salted shoulder of pork*
- *6 Strasbourg sausages*
- *6 Montbéliard sausages*
- *400 g smoked bacon*
- *400 g salted bacon*
- *3 small ham shanks*
- *6 medium potatoes*

Wash the sauerkraut in cold water, drain and press to get rid of the water.

Wrap the garlic, the bay leaf and the spices in a small piece of muslin and close it using kitchen string.

Slice the onion. Melt the lard in a large casserole and brown the onions. Add half of the sauerkraut, then the pork shoulder, the bacon, the ham shanks and the bag of spices. Cover with the remaining sauerkraut. Moisten with the white wine and add water to cover. Lightly season.

Cook on a low heat with the lid on for 1½ hours, checking that there is always some liquid in the bottom of the casserole.

Peel the potatoes. Place them on top of the sauerkraut 30 minutes before the end of the cooking time.

Bring a saucepan of water to the boil. When boiling, add the Strasbourg and Montbéliard sausages, cover and take off the heat. Leave in the hot water for 10 to 15 minutes.

Info: Sauerkraut is best eaten while it still has some bite, white or slightly golden and caught on the bottom of the casserole depending on your preference.

Drinks: White wine from Alsace or beer.

Definition:

Moisten: add liquid.

Tip: Make a sauerkraut pie with the leftovers.

Tarte Flambée

Serves 4

For the dough
- *500 g flour*
- *250 g water*
- *10 g yeast*
- *2 tbsp oil*
- *1 pinch of salt*

For the cream
- *1 kg 0% fromage blanc*
- *½ l crème fraîche*
- *10 cl rapeseed oil*
- *1 egg*
- *½ teaspoon garlic powder*
- *Salt, pepper*
- *1 pinch of nutmeg*

For the topping
- *2 onions*
- *300 g bacon*

Dilute the yeast in a little tepid water.

Sieve the flour, make a well in it and add the remaining ingredients for the dough.

Knead together until you have a smooth dough. Shape into a ball, cover with a cloth and leave to prove for 1 hour.

Whisk all the ingredients for the cream together.

Slice the onions.

Cut the bacon into very fine lardons.

Take 200 g of dough and roll it out into a rectangle as finely as possible.

Spread a ladleful of the cream on the rolled out dough and scatter with onions and lardons.

Bake for 3-4 minutes in a hot oven, 250°C, thermostat 8.

Serving suggestion: with a green salad.

Variant: Add sliced mushrooms or grated Gruyere…

Kassler

Preparation: 15 min
Cooking: 30 min

Serves 4

- 800 g kassler or smoked ham
- 1 onion
- 4 cloves
- 2 cloves of garlic
- 2 carrots
- 1 bouquet garni

Peel the carrots, the garlic and the onion.

Stick the cloves into the onion.

Put the meat and the other ingredients in saucepan. Cover with water

Bring to the boil and cook over a low heat for 35 minutes.

Serving suggestion: Potato salad.

Cocotte au munster

Munster casserole

Preparation: 15 min
Cooking: 20 min

Serves 4

- *1 Munster cheese weighing 450 g*
- *20 cl crème fleurette*
- *20 cl Gewurztraminer*
- *Pepper*

Cut the Munster into small pieces.

Divide it between 4 individual casserole dishes.

Add the wine and the cream. Season with pepper.

Bake for 15 minutes at 200°C, thermostat 6.5.

Serving suggestion: Green salad and sauté potatoes

Definition:

Crème fleurette: Liquid cream with 35% fat.

Croustillant de pied de porc
Crispy pig's trotter

Preparation: 1½ hours
Cooking: 2½ hours
Resting time: 12 hours

Serves 6

- 2 pig's trotters
- 1 l red wine
- 50 cl water
- 1 tbsp Patrelle flavouring (optional)
- 1 bouquet garni
- 1 clove of garlic
- 10 g tomato paste
- Salt, coarsely crushed white peppercorns

- 300 g sauerkraut
- ½ onion
- 10 cl white wine
- 20 g shallots
- 500 g pig's caul
- 12 sheets of filo pastry
- 100 g cooked salted belly pork

Put the pig's trotters, the wine, the water, the Patrelle flavouring, the bouquet garni, the garlic and the tomato paste in a large saucepan. Season and mix.

Cook covered over a low heat until the meat comes away from the bone. Around 2 hours.

Peel and slice the onion. Soften it in a teaspoon of oil.

Add the sauerkraut, the white wine and the water to just cover the cabbage and cook over a low heat for 1 hour.

Put a sheet of greaseproof paper in the bottom of a dish.

While still hot, bone the pig's trotters and flatten the flesh in the dish lined with greaseproof paper.

Leave to harden in the fridge for 12 hours.

When the pig's trotters have hardened, cut them into small pieces, 2 x 2 cm.

Chop the shallots and cut the cooked belly pork into small pieces.

Brown the shallots and the belly pork in a tablespoon of oil.

Mix the diced pig's trotters, the sauerkraut, the shallots and the belly pork.

Divide your mixture into 12 identical portions.

Shape each portion into a cylinder and wrap it tightly in caul and then in a sheet of filo pastry.

Grease an oven tray and place the cylinders on it.

Bake at 180°C, thermostat 6, for 10 minutes.

Serving suggestion: Green salad

Definition:

Line: Cover the bottom of a mould.

Jambonneau au munster
Knuckle of ham with Munster

**Preparation: 25 min
Cooking: 2½ hours**

Serves 6

• 6 jambonneaux or
salted knuckles of ham

• 50 cl red wine

• 20 cl veal stock

• 300 g Munster

• 20 cl crème fleurette

• Salt, pepper

Season the knuckles. In a hot casserole, brown the knuckles on each side and moisten with the veal stock and the wine.

Bake for 2½ hours at 150°C, thermostat 5.

Check that they are cooked. The knuckle should be split.

Bring the crème fleurette to the boil and remove from the heat.

Add the diced Munster and mix until the cream is smooth.

Serve.

Definition:

Crème fleurette: *Liquid cream with 35% fat.*

Serving suggestion: *Sauté potatoes.*

Tête de veau sauce gribiche

Calf's head with ~~gribiche~~ sauce

g: 2¾ hours
Soaking: 2 hours

6

Serves 6

For the meat
- *1.5 kg calf's head*
- *500 g veal tongue*
- *6 carrots*
- *2 leeks*
- *2 onions*
- *1 pinch nitrite pickling salt or pink salt*

For the accompaniment
- *6 large gherkins*
- *1 tomato*
- *6 eggs*
- *6 teaspoons capers*
- *24 black olives*
- *2 onions*

For the gribiche sauce
- *5 cl vinegar*
- *15 cl oil*
- *1 tbsp mustard condiment*
- *2 gherkins*
- *1 teaspoon capers*
- *1 shallot*
- *2 eggs*
- *Salt, pepper*

Clean the veal tongue, remove the glands.

Put the calf's head and tongue in a large quantity of water with a pinch of nitrite pickling salt and bring to the boil.

Refresh, remove the skin from the tongue and cut the meat into large pieces.

Peel the carrots and cut them into 2-cm slices.

Clean the leeks and cut them into 10-cm slices.

Quarter the onions.

Put the meat, the vegetables and the bouquet garni in a large casserole. Cover with water, cover the casserole and cook for 2 hours over a low heat.

Preparing the gribiche sauce

Bring a saucepan of water to the boil to cook 2 hardboiled eggs. Drop the eggs into the boiling water and cook for 9 minutes. Refresh them and shell them.

Finely chop the shallot, the gherkins and the hardboiled eggs.

Mix the oil, the vinegar, the mustard and the salt and pepper.

Add the chopped shallot, gherkins and eggs. Mix.

When cooked, present on a serving dish with the accompaniment and serve with the gribiche sauce.

Info: The nitrite pickling salt or pink salt allow the meat to retain its pink colour.

Definition:

Shell: remove the shell from the hardboiled eggs.

Coquelet au Riesling
Cockerel in Riesling

Preparation: 30 min
Cooking: 30 min

Serves 6

- *3 young cockerels*
- *400 g mushrooms*
- *200 g button onions*
- *150 g lardons*
- *50 cl white wine (Riesling)*
- *50 cl liquid cream*
- *50 cl chicken stock*
- *10 cl oil*
- *50 g butter*

Peel the onions and quarter the mushrooms.

Heat the oil and the butter in a casserole. Brown the young cockerels on each side and on the back and the breast. Put the cockerels to one side and remove the excess fat from the casserole.

Brown the onions, the mushrooms and the lardons. Lightly season.

Deglaze with the white wine, add the chicken stock, the cream and the cockerels.

Cover and cook for 30 minutes over a low heat.

Check that the cockerels are cooked. To do this, prick the cockerels and tilt them. If the juices run out clear, the cockerels are cooked. If there is still any blood in the juices, cook a little longer.

Serving suggestion: Spaetzle.

Joues de porc confites
Braised pork cheeks

Preparation: 1 hour
Cooking: 3 hours
Brine: 24 hours

Serves 6

- 1.5 kg pork cheeks
- 1 kg goose fat

For the brine
- 2 bay leaves
- 30 g coarse salt
- 2 cloves of garlic
- 6 juniper berries
- 2 cloves

For the horseradish cream
- 50 g horseradish
- 20 cl liquid cream
- 10 cl veal stock

The day before

Put the pork cheeks, the goose fat and the other ingredients in the brine in a large casserole.

Mix, cover and put in the fridge for 24 hours.

On the day

Put the casserole over a low heat and cook for 3 hours.

Mix all the ingredients for the cream.

When cooked, serve the pork cheeks with the horseradish cream.

Tip: If you can't get goose fat, use lard.

Roosbif

Serves 6

- *2 kg horse loin*
- *50 g carrots*
- *50 g leeks*
- *50 g onions*
- *3 cloves of garlic*
- *1 bouquet garni*
- *20 g coarsely ground white pepper*
- *2 l red wine*
- *1 tbsp oil*
- *50 g flour*

3 days before

Peel the carrots and clean the leek and cut them into rounds.

Peel and slice the onion.

Put the meat, the vegetables, the coarsely ground pepper and the wine in a salad bowl.

Marinate in the fridge for 72 hours.

On the day

Drain the meat and the vegetables. Save the marinade.

Heat a tablespoon of oil in a casserole and brown the meat on all sides.

Remove the meat and add the vegetables. Let them sweat.

Return the meat to the casserole, sprinkle with 50 g of flour and moisten with the marinade.

Add the bouquet garni and the garlic. Season.

Cook the meat covered over a low heat for 2½ hours.

Slice the meat finely and dress with the sauce.

Serving suggestion: Potato salad.

Tourte à la choucroute
Sauerkraut pie

Preparation: 30 min
Cooking: 45 min

Serves 6

- I kg cooked sauerkraut cabbage
- 500 g cooked sauerkraut meat (sausages, frankfurters, bacon, smoked ham, etc.)
- 2 sheets of puff pastry
- 2 eggs

Cut the meat and the sausages into pieces.

Mix the cabbage, the pieces of meat and an egg.

Spread the mixture over one sheet of pastry and cover with the other sheet.

Brush the edges of the pastry with egg yolk and press with your fingers to seal.

Make a hole in the middle of the pie.

Brush the puff pastry with egg yolk.

Bake at 180°C, thermostat 6, for 45 minutes.

Tip: Dress with sauerkraut leftovers.

Serving suggestion: Green salad.

Pot au feu

Preparation: 30 min
Cooking: 2½ hours

Serves 6

- 500 g beef top rib
- 500 g beef brisket
- I kg chuck steak
- 3 marrowbones
- I onion
- I bouquet garni
- I small white cabbage
- 6 carrots
- I celery stalk
- 4 leeks
- 2 yellow turnips
- I clove

Peel the carrots, the celery and the turnips.

Cut the carrots into 4-cm slices. Quarter the turnips and cut the celery into pieces.

Stick a clove into an unpeeled onion.

Put the meat and the other ingredients in large saucepan. Cover with water and bring to the boil. Season.

Skim off the scum that forms on the surface.

Cook for 2½ hours and serve.

Tip: Make a large quantity of pot au feu to make a pot au feu salad or fleichnakas with the leftovers.

Quenelles de foie
Liver dumplings

Preparation: 15 min
Cooking: 30 min
Soaking: 24 hours

Serves 6

- 500 g pig's liver
- 125 g smoked bacon
- 250 g veal suet (kidney fat)
- 150 g semolina
- 30 g parsley
- 2 eggs
- Salt, pepper
- 50 g butter

Mix the liver, the bacon, the onion, the parsley and the fat in a food processor.

Add the eggs and the semolina and season.

Mix with a spatula to get a smooth mixture.

Shape the dumplings using 2 tablespoons.

Bring 3 litres of salted water to the boil.

Poach the dumplings for 10 minutes. As soon as they rise to the surface, drain them and keep warm until you are ready to serve.

Serving suggestion: Green salad and sauté potatoes.

Carpe frite
Fried carp

Preparation: 30 min
Cooking: 20 min

Serves 6

- 1 carp
- 3 eggs
- 150 g semolina
- Salt, pepper
- 3 lemons

Scale and gut the carp.

Cut it into slices 2 cm thick.

Salt and leave to rest for 20 minutes.

Dry with kitchen paper.

Heat a deep fat fryer.

Beat the eggs. Season.

Dredge the slices of carp in the egg and then in the semolina.

Cook them in the deep fat fryer for 10 minutes.

Serve immediately accompanied with lemon quarters.

Serving suggestion: Steamed potatoes, green salad, mayonnaise.

Matelote de poissons
Fish stew

**Preparation: 1 ½ hours
Cooking: 20 min**

Serves 6

- 500 g pike
- 500 g zander
- 1 kg eels
- 200 g button onions
- 300 g mushrooms
- 50 cl white wine
- 50 cl crème fraîche
- 1 egg yolk

Scale, gut and cut your fish into steaks 4 cm thick.

Slice the mushrooms.

Panfry your pieces of fish in butter for 3 minutes on each side.

Deglaze with white wine and put the fish in a warm oven at 60°C, thermostat 2.

Add the onions, the mushrooms and the cream to the pan. Season.

Reduce by half and bind the sauce with the egg yolk.

Arrange the fish on a serving dish and pour over the sauce.

Serving suggestion: Fine noodles or tagliatelle.

Sandre au Riesling
Zander in Riesling

Preparation: 20 min
Cooking: 20 min

Serves 4

- 4 zander fillets
- 1 shallot
- 100 g mushrooms
- 30 cl white wine (Riesling)
- 30 cl crème fraîche
- 50 g butter
- 30 cl fish stock
- 3 tbsp flour
- Salt, pepper

Slice the shallot and the mushrooms.

Flour the fish on each side.

Melt half of the butter in a casserole dish that can be used on top of the stove and in the oven. Slightly colour the fillets on both sides. Put to one side.

Add the remaining butter and sweat the shallots and mushrooms.

Place the fish on top, deglaze with white wine, and add the fish stock and the cream. Season.

Bake in a hot oven at 180°C, thermostat 6, for 10 minutes.

Put the fish into a serving dish. Reduce the cooking juices if necessary until they coat the back of a spoon.

Pour over the fish.

Definition:

Deglaze: dissolve the juices caramelised during cooking with a liquid.

Sweat: allow the ingredients to release their water.

Serving suggestion: Accompany with fine noodles or steamed potatoes.

Wine: Riesling.

Choucroute au poisson
Sauerkraut with fish

**Preparation: 30 min
Cooking: 1 ½ hours**

Serves 6

- 1.2 kg sauerkraut cabbage
- 1 onion
- 10 g powdered cinnamon
- 10 cl white wine
- 12 potatoes
- 10 cl oil
- 6 large mussels
- 6 red mullet fillets
- 6 x 100 g smoked haddock
- 6 x 100 g zander
- 6 scallops
- 6 large prawns

For the beurre blanc:
- 50 g shallots
- 20 cl white wine
- 200 g butter
- Salt, pepper

Mix the sauerkraut cabbage and the cinnamon.

Peel and slice the onion.

In a saucepan, heat a tablespoon of oil and brown the sliced onion.

Add the sauerkraut, just cover with water and cook over a low heat for 1 ½ hours.

After an hour, add the peeled potatoes.

After an hour and 20 minutes of cooking, add the haddock.

Meanwhile, heat the oil in a frying pan and cook the zander and the red mullet on one side only for 7 minutes and panfry the prawns and the scallops for 2 minutes on each side.

For the beurre blanc

Peel and slice the shallots and sweat them in 50 g of butter. Do not allow to colour.

Moisten with the white wine and reduce by half.

Add the rest of the butter and emulsify in a blender.

Cordon bleu de Sandre
Zander cordon bleu

Preparation: 20 min
Cooking: 45 min

Serves 6

- 6 180-g zander steaks with the skin
- 6 thin slices of bacon
- 6 thin slices of Gruyere

For the coating
- 4 tbsp flour
- 1 egg
- 4 tbsp powdered almond

For the sauce
- 150 g shallots
- 50 cl pinot noir
- 30 g margarine
- 30 cl veal stock
- 20 cl Noilly Prat
- 100 g butter

Chop the shallots and sweat in a tablespoon of oil.

Moisten with the wine, the Noilly Prat and the stock. Reduce by half.

Add the diced butter. Blend and pass through the chinois.

Cut the zander in two to form a kind of wallet.

Lay the slices of bacon and Gruyere on top. Close again.

Dust every side of the zander with flour, and then dip in the beaten egg and finally the powdered almond.

Quickly brown the zander on both sides in a hot, oiled frying pan.

Finish cooking in the oven at 180°C, thermostat 6, for 10 minutes.

Serving suggestion: steamed potatoes.

Definition:

Chinois: very fine sieve used to filter liquids.

Moisten: add liquid.

Sweat: allow the ingredients to release their water.

Spaetzle

Preparation: 20 min
Cooking: 5 min

Combine all the ingredients with a wooden spatula until evenly mixed.

Shape the spaetzle with a spaetzle grater or by cutting them into small pieces 3 cm long by 5 mm wide.

Bring a large quantity of water to the boil.

Drop the spaetzle into the water and take them out as soon as they rise to the surface.

Spaetzle can also be sautéed after cooking.

Serves 6
- 500 g fine white flour
- 5 eggs
- 25 cl milk
- Nutmeg
- Salt, pepper

Quenelles de fromage blanc
Fromage blanc dumplings

Preparation: 20 min
Cooking: 10 min

Combine all the ingredients except the flour with a wooden spatula until evenly mixed.

Make dumplings with the mixture using two tablespoons.

Bring a large quantity of water to the boil in a saucepan.

Drop the dumplings into the boiling water. When they rise the surface, allow 5 minutes additional cooking time.

Take them out of the water with a slotted spoon and put them in a bowl of iced water.

Put them to one side on a dry cloth and let them dry for 15 minutes.

Roll the dumplings in the breadcrumbs and sauté them in a tablespoon of oil.

Tip: The fine white flour can be replaced by sieved flour.

Serves 6
- 250 g fromage blanc
- 500 g fine white flour
- 5 eggs
- Nutmeg
- Breadcrumbs
- Salt, pepper

Dampfnudel

Preparation: 1½ hours
Rising time: 5 hours
Cooking: 10 min

Serves 6

- *400 g flour*
- *18 cl milk*
- *15 g sugar*
- *2 eggs*
- *60 g softened butter*
- *10 g yeast*
- *10 cl peanut oil*

Make a well in the flour. Add the milk, the sugar, the beaten eggs and the crumbled yeast. Knead the dough, folding it back on itself, until thoroughly mixed. Incorporate the softened butter and knead until the dough is smooth and evenly mixed.

Put the dough in a salad bowl and keep in a warm place. When it has doubled in volume, around 2 hours, knead again and leave it to double in volume again.

Knead the dough and roll out a rectangle 2 cm thick. Cut out rounds with an 8-cm pastry cutter. Leave to rest and double in volume.

In a casserole, heat the oil and brown the dampfnudels on each side. Add 10 cl of water and cook for 4 minutes.

Salade de pommes de terre
Potato salad

Preparation: 20 min
Cooking: 20 min

Serves 6

- *1.5 kg firm-fleshed medium-sized potatoes (such as Charlotte)*
- *150 g onions*

For the vinaigrette

- *1 tbsp mustard condiment*
- *1 egg yolk*
- *3 tbsp vinegar*
- *6 tbsp oil*
- *15 cl white wine*
- *Salt, pepper*

Boil the potatoes in water with 10 g of salt. Leave to cool.

Peel the onions and sweat in a tablespoon of oil.

Peel the potatoes and cut them into rounds.

Mix the ingredients for the vinaigrette and add the potatoes and the onions. Mix and serve.

Tips: Add parsley or olives.

Auteurs
Didier Roeckel et l'équipe du Restaurant de la Couronne d'Or à Scherwiller

Photographe
Frédérique Clément
www.fredclement.com

Maquette
I.D. Créations, Damien Schitter

Relecture
Marie Heckmann et Antoine Dounovetz

I.D. l'Édition

9, rue des Artisans - 67210 Bernardswiller
Tél. : 03 88 34 22 00 - Fax : 03 88 34 26 26
id.edition@wanadoo.fr - www.id-edition.com

ISBN : 978-2-915626-98-8
Impression : Arti Grafiche (Pomezia)
juillet 2013